A JAMES CAMERON FILM

TITANIC

PARAMOUNT PICTURES AND TWENTIETH CENTURY FOX PRESENT A LIGHTSTORM ENTERTAINMENT PRODUCTION A JAMES CAMERON FILM "TITANIC" LEONARDO DiCAPRIO KATE WINSLET BILLY ZANE KATHY BATES FRANCES FISHER BERNARD HILL JONATHAN HYDE DANNY NUCCI GLORIA STUART DAVID WARNER AND BILL PAXTON MUSIC BY JAMES HORNER COSTUME DESIGNER DEBORAH L. SCOTT MUSIC SUPERVISOR RANDY GERSTON CO-PRODUCERS AL GIDDINGS GRANT HILL SHARON MANN FILM EDITORS CONRAD BUFF, A.C.E. JAMES CAMERON RICHARD A. HARRIS PRODUCTION DESIGNER PETER LAMONT DIRECTOR OF PHOTOGRAPHY RUSSELL CARPENTER, A.S.C. SPECIAL VISUAL EFFECTS BY DIGITAL DOMAIN EXECUTIVE PRODUCER RAE SANCHINI PRODUCED BY JAMES CAMERON AND JON LANDAU

Soundtrack Available on SONY CLASSICAL   Read the book by HARPERPERENNIAL   WRITTEN AND DIRECTED BY JAMES CAMERON   titanicmovie.com

Featuring "My Heart Will Go On" Performed by Celine Dion

PG-13 PARENTS STRONGLY CAUTIONED — Some Material May Be Inappropriate for Children Under 13

*TWENTIETH CENTURY FOX. COPYRIGHT © 1998 BY PARAMOUNT PICTURES AND TWENTIETH CENTURY FOX. ALL RIGHTS RESERVED.

ISBN 0-7935-9224-0

HAL•LEONARD®
CORPORATION

7777 W. BLUEMOUND RD. P.O. BOX 13819 MILWAUKEE, WI 53213

Visit Hal Leonard Online at
www.halleonard.com

NEVER AN ABSOLUTION

By JAMES HORNER

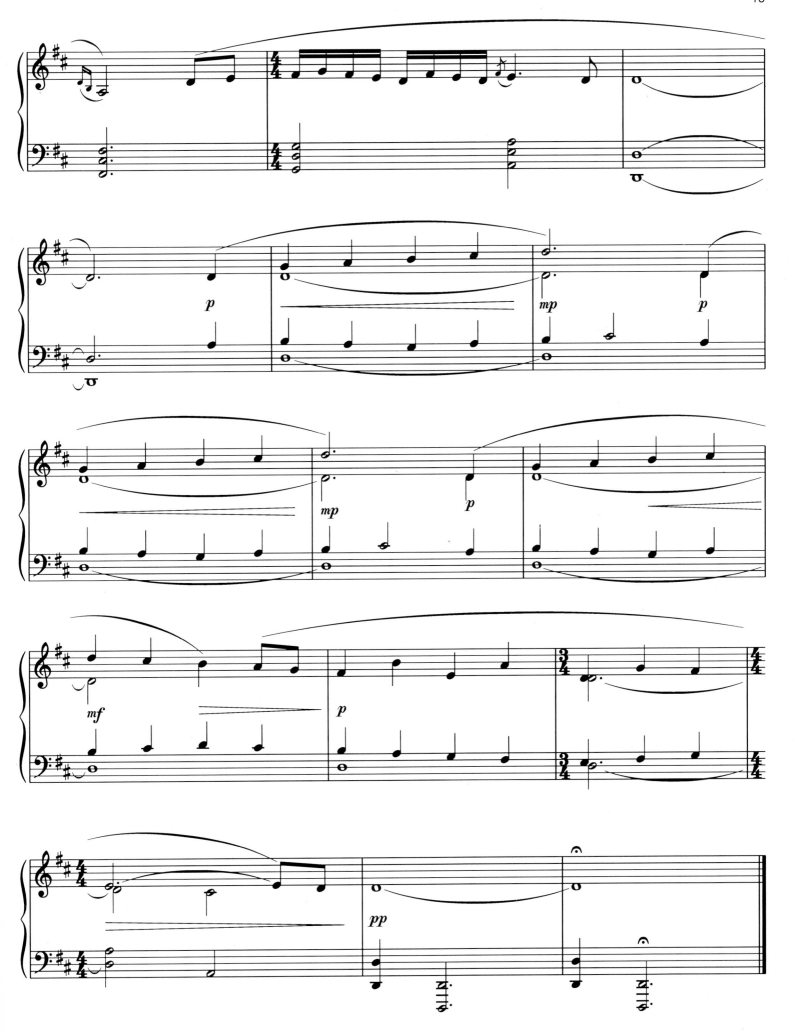

SOUTHAMPTON

By JAMES HORNER

ROSE

By JAMES HORNER

Moderately, flowing

"TAKE HER TO SEA, MR. MURDOCH"

By JAMES HORNER

"HARD TO STARBOARD"

By JAMES HORNER

34

8vb _____

UNABLE TO STAY, UNWILLING TO LEAVE

By JAMES HORNER

Driving beat

Play 3 times

HYMN TO THE SEA

By JAMES HORNER

MY HEART WILL GO ON

(Love Theme from 'Titanic')

Music by JAMES HORNER
Lyric by WILL JENNINGS